MW01234809

TO:

_____

FROM:

_____

DATE:

_____

*"Come to me, all of you who are weary
and burdened, and I will give you rest."*
~Matthew 11:28~

Don't worry about anything, but in everything,
through prayer and petition with thanksgiving,
present your requests to God.
~Philippians 4:6~

Rejoice always, pray constantly, give thanks in everything;
for this is God's will for you in Christ Jesus.
~1 Thessalonians 5:16-18~

*Be strong and courageous; don't be terrified
or afraid of them. For the L*ORD* your God is the one who
will go with you; he will not leave you or abandon you.
~Deuteronomy 31:6~*

*Let us run with endurance the race that lies
before us, keeping our eyes on Jesus,
the source and perfecter of our faith.
~Hebrews 12:1-2~*

*Take delight in the LORD, and he will
give you your heart's desires.
~Psalm 37:4~*

*"Love the Lord your God with all your heart,
with all your soul, and with all your mind."*
~Matthew 22:37~

*And be kind and compassionate to
one another, forgiving one another, just
as God also forgave you in Christ.
~Ephesians 4:32~*

*For you are saved by grace through faith,
and this is not from yourselves; it is God's gift—
not from works, so that no one can boast.
~Ephesians 2:8–9~*

I have been crucified with Christ,
and I no longer live, but Christ lives in me.
~Galatians 2:20~

*For we are his workmanship, created in
Christ Jesus for good works, which God
prepared ahead of time for us to do.
~Ephesians 2:10~*

The one who walks with the wise will become wise,
but a companion of fools will suffer harm.
~Proverbs 13:20~

"Haven't I commanded you: be strong and courageous? Do not be afraid or discouraged, for the LORD your God is with you wherever you go."
~Joshua 1:9~

Trust in the LORD forever, because in the LORD,
the LORD himself, is an everlasting rock!
~Isaiah 26:4~

*Do nothing out of selfish ambition
or conceit, but in humility consider others
as more important than yourselves.*
~Philippians 2:3~

Blessed is the one who endures trials, because
when he has stood the test he will receive the crown
of life that God has promised to those who love him.
~James 1:12~

Because of the Lord's faithful love we do not perish, for his mercies never end. They are new every morning; great is your faithfulness!
~Lamentations 3:22-23~

_____

Therefore we do not give up. Even though
our outer person is being destroyed, our inner
person is being renewed day by day.
~2 Corinthians 4:16~

*Do not be conformed to this age, but be transformed
by the renewing of your mind, so that you may discern
what is the good, pleasing, and perfect will of God.
~Romans 12:2~*

Trust in the Lord with all your heart,
and do not rely on your own understanding.
~Proverbs 3:5~

*For the word of God is living and effective and sharper
than any double-edged sword, penetrating as far as
the separation of soul and spirit, joints and marrow. It is able
to judge the thoughts and intentions of the heart.
~Hebrews 4:12~*

The Lord does not delay his promise, as some
understand delay, but is patient with you, not wanting
any to perish but all to come to repentance.
~2 Peter 3:9~

*"The Lᴏʀᴅ your God is among you, a warrior who saves.
He will rejoice over you with gladness. He will be
quiet in his love. He will delight in you with singing."*
~Zephaniah 3:17~

_____

But I know that my Redeemer lives,
and at the end he will stand on the dust.
~Job 19:25~

*"Come to me, all of you who are weary
and burdened, and I will give you rest."*
~Matthew 11:28~

*Don't worry about anything, but in everything,
through prayer and petition with thanksgiving,
present your requests to God.*
~Philippians 4:6~

*Rejoice always, pray constantly, give thanks in everything;
for this is God's will for you in Christ Jesus.
~1 Thessalonians 5:16-18~*

Be strong and courageous; don't be terrified
or afraid of them. For the Lord _your God is the one who_
will go with you; he will not leave you or abandon you."
~Deuteronomy 31:6~

*Let us run with endurance the race that lies
before us, keeping our eyes on Jesus,
the source and perfecter of our faith.
~Hebrews 12:1-2~*

*Take delight in the LORD, and he will
give you your heart's desires.
~Psalm 37:4~*

"Love the Lord your God with all your heart,
with all your soul, and with all your mind."
~Matthew 22:37~

_And be kind and compassionate to
one another, forgiving one another, just
as God also forgave you in Christ._
~Ephesians 4:32~

*For you are saved by grace through faith,
and this is not from yourselves; it is God's gift—
not from works, so that no one can boast.
~Ephesians 2:8-9~*

I have been crucified with Christ,
and I no longer live, but Christ lives in me.
~Galatians 2:20~

For we are his workmanship, created in
Christ Jesus for good works, which God
prepared ahead of time for us to do.
~Ephesians 2:10~

The one who walks with the wise will become wise,
but a companion of fools will suffer harm.
~Proverbs 13:20~

*"Haven't I commanded you: be strong and
courageous? Do not be afraid or discouraged,
for the Lᴏʀᴅ your God is with you wherever you go."
~Joshua 1:9~*

_____

Trust in the LORD forever, because in the LORD,
the LORD himself, is an everlasting rock!
~Isaiah 26:4~

*Do nothing out of selfish ambition
or conceit, but in humility consider others
as more important than yourselves.
~Philippians 2:3~*

*Blessed is the one who endures trials, because
when he has stood the test he will receive the crown
of life that God has promised to those who love him.
~James 1:12~*

Because of the Lord's faithful love we do not perish, for his mercies never end. They are new every morning; great is your faithfulness!
~Lamentations 3:22-23~

Therefore we do not give up. Even though our outer person is being destroyed, our inner person is being renewed day by day.
~2 Corinthians 4:16~

*Do not be conformed to this age, but be transformed
by the renewing of your mind, so that you may discern
what is the good, pleasing, and perfect will of God.
~Romans 12:2~*

Trust in the Lord with all your heart,
and do not rely on your own understanding.
~Proverbs 3:5~

For the word of God is living and effective and sharper
than any double-edged sword, penetrating as far as
the separation of soul and spirit, joints and marrow. It is able
to judge the thoughts and intentions of the heart.
~Hebrews 4:12~

_____

The Lord does not delay his promise, as some
understand delay, but is patient with you, not wanting
any to perish but all to come to repentance.
~2 Peter 3:9~

*"The LORD your God is among you, a warrior who saves.
He will rejoice over you with gladness. He will be
quiet in his love. He will delight in you with singing."
~Zephaniah 3:17~*

But I know that my Redeemer lives,
and at the end he will stand on the dust.
~Job 19:25~

*"Come to me, all of you who are weary
and burdened, and I will give you rest."*
~Matthew 11:28~

Don't worry about anything, but in everything,
through prayer and petition with thanksgiving,
present your requests to God.
~Philippians 4:6~

Rejoice always, pray constantly, give thanks in everything;
for this is God's will for you in Christ Jesus.
~1 Thessalonians 5:16-18~

*Be strong and courageous; don't be terrified
or afraid of them. For the L*ORD *your God is the one who
will go with you; he will not leave you or abandon you."
~Deuteronomy 31:6~*

Let us run with endurance the race that lies
before us, keeping our eyes on Jesus,
the source and perfecter of our faith.
~Hebrews 12:1-2~

*Take delight in the LORD, and he will
give you your heart's desires.
~Psalm 37:4~*

*"Love the Lord your God with all your heart,
with all your soul, and with all your mind."*
~Matthew 22:37~

*And be kind and compassionate to
one another, forgiving one another, just
as Go also forgave you in Christ.
~Ephesians 4:32~*

*For you are saved by grace through faith,
and this is not from yourselves; it is God's gift—
not from works, so that no one can boast.
~Ephesians 2:8-9~*

I have been crucified with Christ,
and I no longer live, but Christ lives in me.
~Galatians 2:20~

For we are his workmanship, created in Christ Jesus for good works, which God prepared ahead of time for us to do.
~Ephesians 2:10~

The one who walks with the wise will become wise,
but a companion of fools will suffer harm.
~Proverbs 13:20~

"Haven't I commanded you: be strong and courageous? Do not be afraid or discouraged, for the LORD your God is with you wherever you go."
~Joshua 1:9~

_Trust in the L_ORD _forever, because in the L_ORD,
_the L_ORD _himself, is an everlasting rock!_
~Isaiah 26:4~

Do nothing out of selfish ambition
or conceit, but in humility consider others
as more important than yourselves.
~Philippians 2:3~

Blessed is the one who endures trials, because
when he has stood the test he will receive the crown
of life that God has promised to those who love him.
~James 1:12~

Because of the Lord's faithful love we do not perish, for his mercies never end. They are new every morning; great is your faithfulness!
~Lamentations 3:22-23~

Therefore we do not give up. Even though
our outer person is being destroyed, our inner
person is being renewed day by day.
~2 Corinthians 4:16~

Do not be conformed to this age, but be transformed
by the renewing of your mind, so that you may discern
what is the good, pleasing, and perfect will of God.
~Romans 12:2~

Trust in the LORD with all your heart,
and do not rely on your own understanding.
~Proverbs 3:5~

For the word of God is living and effective and sharper
than any double-edged sword, penetrating as far as
the separation of soul and spirit, joints and marrow. It is able
to judge the thoughts and intentions of the heart.
~Hebrews 4:12~

*The Lord does not delay his promise, as some
understand delay, but is patient with you, not wanting
any to perish but all to come to repentance.
~2 Peter 3:9~*

*"The Lord your God is among you, a warrior who saves.
He will rejoice over you with gladness. He will be
quiet in his love. He will delight in you with singing."*
~Zephaniah 3:17~

But I know that my Redeemer lives,
and at the end he will stand on the dust.
~Job 19:25~

*"Come to me, all of you who are weary
and burdened, and I will give you rest."*
~Matthew 11:28~

Don't worry about anything, but in everything,
through prayer and petition with thanksgiving,
present your requests to God.
~Philippians 4:6~

Rejoice always, pray constantly, give thanks in everything;
for this is God's will for you in Christ Jesus.
~1 Thessalonians 5:16–18~

Be strong and courageous; don't be terrified
_or afraid of them. For the L_ord _your God is the one who_
will go with you; he will not leave you or abandon you."
~Deuteronomy 31:6~

Let us run with endurance the race that lies
before us, keeping our eyes on Jesus,
the source and perfecter of our faith.
~Hebrews 12:1-2~

*Take delight in the LORD, and he will
give you your heart's desires.
~Psalm 37:4~*

_"Love the Lord your God with all your heart,
with all your soul, and with all your mind."_
~Matthew 22:37~

*And be kind and compassionate to
one another, forgiving one another, just
as God also forgave you in Christ.
~Ephesians 4:32~*

*For you are saved by grace through faith,
and this is not from yourselves; it is God's gift—
not from works, so that no one can boast.
~Ephesians 2:8-9~*

I have been crucified with Christ,
and I no longer live, but Christ lives in me.
~Galatians 2:20~

*For we are his workmanship, created in
Christ Jesus for good works, which God
prepared ahead of time for us to do.
~Ephesians 2:10~*

_____

The one who walks with the wise will become wise,
but a companion of fools will suffer harm.
~Proverbs 13:20~

*"Haven't I commanded you: be strong and
courageous? Do not be afraid or discouraged,
for the L*ORD *your God is with you wherever you go."
~Joshua 1:9~*

_Trust in the Lᴏʀᴅ forever, because in the Lᴏʀᴅ,
the Lᴏʀᴅ himself, is an everlasting rock!
~Isaiah 26:4~_

*Do nothing out of selfish ambition
or conceit, but in humility consider others
as more important than yourselves.
~Philippians 2:3~*

*Blessed is the one who endures trials, because
when he has stood the test he will receive the crown
of life that God has promised to those who love him.
~James 1:12~*

Because of the Lord's faithful love we do not perish, for his mercies never end. They are new every morning; great is your faithfulness!
~Lamentations 3:22-23~

Therefore we do not give up. Even though our outer person is being destroyed, our inner person is being renewed day by day.
~2 Corinthians 4:16~

*Do not be conformed to this age, but be transformed
by the renewing of your mind, so that you may discern
what is the good, pleasing, and perfect will of God.
~Romans 12:2~*

Trust in the Lord _with all your heart,_
and do not rely on your own understanding.
~Proverbs 3:5~

*For the word of God is living and effective and sharper
than any double-edged sword, penetrating as far as
the separation of soul and spirit, joints and marrow. It is able
to judge the thoughts and intentions of the heart.
~Hebrews 4:12~*

The Lord does not delay his promise, as some understand delay, but is patient with you, not wanting any to perish but all to come to repentance.
~2 Peter 3:9~

*"The LORD your God is among you, a warrior who saves.
He will rejoice over you with gladness. He will be quiet
in his love. He will delight in you with singing."*
~Zephaniah 3:17~

But I know that my Redeemer lives,
and at the end he will stand on the dust.
~Job 19:25~

*"Come to me, all of you who are weary
and burdened, and I will give you rest."*
~Matthew 11:28~

_Don't worry about anything, but in everything,
through prayer and petition with thanksgiving,
present your requests to God.
~Philippians 4:6~_

Rejoice always, pray constantly, give thanks in everything;
for this is God's will for you in Christ Jesus.
~1 Thessalonians 5:16–18~

Be strong and courageous; don't be terrified
or afraid of them. For the LORD your God is the one who
will go with you; he will not leave you or abandon you.
~Deuteronomy 31:6~

*Let us run with endurance the race that lies
before us, keeping our eyes on Jesus,
the source and perfecter of our faith.
~Hebrews 12:1-2~*

Take delight in the Lord, and he will
give you your heart's desires.
~Psalm 37:4~

"Love the Lord your God with all your heart,
with all your soul, and with all your mind."
~Matthew 22:37~

*And be kind and compassionate to
one another, forgiving one another, just
as God also forgave you in Christ.
~Ephesians 4:32~*

For you are saved by grace through faith,
and this is not from yourselves; it is God's gift—
not from works, so that no one can boast.
~Ephesians 2:8-9~

I have been crucified with Christ,
and I no longer live, but Christ lives in me.
~Galatians 2:20~

For we are his workmanship, created in
Christ Jesus for good works, which God
prepared ahead of time for us to do.
~Ephesians 2:10~

The one who walks with the wise will become wise,
but a companion of fools will suffer harm.
~Proverbs 13:20~

*"Haven't I commanded you: be strong and
courageous? Do not be afraid or discouraged,
for the LORD your God is with you wherever you go."
~Joshua 1:9~*

Trust in the Lord forever, because in the Lord,
the Lord himself, is an everlasting rock!.
~Isaiah 26:4~

Do nothing out of selfish ambition
or conceit, but in humility consider others
as more important than yourselves.
~Philippians 2:3~

*Blessed is the one who endures trials, because
when he has stood the test he will receive the crown
of life that God has promised to those who love him.
~James 1:12~*

Because of the Lord's faithful love we do not perish, for his mercies never end. They are new every morning; great is your faithfulness!
~Lamentations 3:22-23~

_____

Therefore we do not give up. Even though
our outer person is being destroyed, our inner
person is being renewed day by day.
~2 Corinthians 4:16~

*Do not be conformed to this age, but be transformed
by the renewing of your mind, so that you may discern
what is the good, pleasing, and perfect will of God.
~Romans 12:2~*

Trust in the Lord with all your heart,
and do not rely on your own understanding.
~Proverbs 3:5~

For the word of God is living and effective and sharper
than any double-edged sword, penetrating as far as
the separation and soul and spirit, joints and marrow. It is able
to judge the thoughts and intentions of the heart.
~Hebrews 4:12~

*The Lord does not delay his promise, as some
understand delay, but is patient with you, not wanting
any to perish but all to come to repentance.*
~2 Peter 3:9~

"The LORD your God is among you, a warrior who saves.
He will rejoice over you with gladness. He will be
quiet in his love. He will delight in you with singing."
~Zephaniah 3:17~

But I know that my Redeemer lives,
and at the end he will stand on the dust.
~Job 19:25~

*"Come to me, all of you who are weary
and burdened, and I will give you rest."*
~Matthew 11:28~

Don't worry about anything, but in everything,
through prayer and petition with thanksgiving,
present your requests to God.
~Philippians 4:6~

*Rejoice always, pray constantly, give thanks in everything;
for this is God's will for you in Christ Jesus.
~1 Thessalonians 5:16–18~*

*Be strong and courageous; don't be terrified
or afraid of them. For the L*ᴏʀᴅ *your God is the one who
will go with you; he will not leave you or abandon you."
~Deuteronomy 31:6~*

Let us run with endurance the race that lies
before us, keeping our eyes on Jesus,
the source and perfecter of our faith.
~Hebrews 12:1-2~

*Take delight in the L ORD, and he will
give you your heart's desires.*
~Psalm 37:4~